PUBLIC SPEAKING

*Storytelling Techniques
For Electrifying Presentations*

Akash P. Karia
No. 1 Internationally Bestselling Author of
"How to Deliver a Great TED Talk" and
"How to Design Ted-Worthy Presentation Slides"
www.AkashKaria.com

Featuring award-winning speeches by:
**Lance Miller, Loghandran Krishnasamy,
Ian Humphrey** and **Erick Rainey**

BESTSELLING BOOKS BY AKASH KARIA

Available on Amazon (www.bit.ly/AkashKaria):

How to Deliver a Great TED Talk

How to Design TED-Worthy Presentation Slides

Own the Room: Presentation Techniques to Keep Your Audience on the Edge of Their Seats

How Successful People Think Differently

ANTI Negativity: How to Stop Negative Thinking and Lead a Positive Life

Persuasion Psychology: 26 Powerful Techniques to Persuade Anyone!

Ready, Set...PROCRASTINATE: 23 Anti-Procrastination Tools Designed to Help You Stop Putting Things off and Start Getting Things Done

FREE RESOURCES

There are hundreds of free articles as well as several eBooks, MP3s and videos on Akash's blog. To get instant access to those, head over to www.AkashKaria.com.

ACKNOWLEDGEMENTS

I would like to extend a huge thank you to all the amazing speakers who kindly given me permission to reprint their speeches in this book. Lance Miller, Loghandran Krishnasamy, Ian Humphrey and Erick Rainey – thank you so much for your support, your guidance and your feedback. This book would not be possible without you. You are not just great speakers, but great mentors!

Thank you also to Craig Valentine (www.CraigValentine.com), whose work and coaching has heavily inspired this book.

Finally, a huge thank you to Toastmasters International (www.Toastmasters.org)– the organization that first got me started on my public speaking journey.

Thank you.

Akash Karia

Author | Speaker | Entrepreneur

RAVE REVIEWS FOR "STORYTELLING TECHNIQUES FOR ELECTRIFYING PRESENTATIONS"

"**A great kick-start for your next speech!** This book provided real examples of great speeches and then broke them down into all the little pieces that came together to make them outstanding. A wonderfully quick burst of inspiration and insight."
~ Mandy Hoffeldt

"A must read! **Akash Karia outlines tips for energizing not only your speech, but also the audience.** He shares his understanding of speech dynamics and helps all readers become better speakers. Anyone who makes presentations should read this book!"
~ Angela Avery

"**Very informative!** The book was informative and the information was "useable" as opposed to complicated and "theory based." The additions of links to actual talks (and then him writing about the talks) was unique and quite helpful."
~ Eric Laughton, Certified John Maxwell coach

"As a professional public speaker, this was so helpful to me. **There were so many tricks of the trade in this book-- like a magician revealing his secrets**. I anticipate using every single tool he describes; in fact, I can hardly wait. It'll bring new life into my presentations."
~ Melissa Reno

"Great resource for speakers. **I have nothing but praise for the simple but succinct way this book reads.** I read it in one sitting and plan to use it as a guide for future speaking engagements."
~ 357 Solutions, LLC

"One of few...This book provides great tips and tools to be an amazing speaker. Easy and enjoyable read! Highly recommended! **Best book to guide you to amazing and memorable speeches.**"
~ Troy Rivera

"**Practical and useful**...Story telling is one of the most important parts of speaking. This book makes it clear how to do it, when and where."
~ Judith Field

"**A must-read for presenters!** Fantastic book on storytelling. Most people don't realize how important storytelling is in good presentations. It's a must have skill set. This is a great resource on the subject."
~ David Bishop

"**Excellent book**...Your public speaking skills will be forever changed."
~ Dongzhe Yang

"Great book...Akash is a very good writer and is very forth coming with information. **He doesn't hold anything back.**"
~ Stephen Fraundorfer

"**Practical. Simple. Clearly-defined strategies.** Quick and easy way to learn and understand key storytelling techniques. Sample speeches with supporting analysis of illustrated techniques were very helpful."
~ M. Y. Moore

"I think this is **a perfect book** to those who want to dominate the art of storytelling."
~ Alci Aguilera

"This book was short and to the point. It is nonetheless **loaded with great advice on how to deliver a killer message.**"
~ David Parra

CONTENTS

YOUR FREE GIFT

As a way of saying thank you for your purchase, I'd like to offer you a free bonus package worth $297. This bonus package contains eBooks, videos and audiotapes on how to overcoming procrastination, mastering the art of persuasion and becoming a good (no, great!) public speaker. You can download the free bonus here:

www.AkashKaria.com/FREE

Dedicated to mum and dad,
Paresh and Nisha Karia,
Because my story
Always begins with you.

CHAPTER ONE

HOW TO BE TWICE THE SPEAKER IN HALF THE TIME

"Speech is power: speech is to persuade, to convert, to compel."
Ralph Waldo Emerson

Have you ever seen a great speaker?

Have you ever seen a boring one?

Have *you* ever been a boring speaker?

What makes the difference between a great speaker and boring one?

To answer this question, I spent the last four years studying and evaluating thousands of speakers - some great ones, and others who (to put it mildly) needed a lot of help. I read over two hundred books on the art of public speaking, storytelling and screenwriting, attended countless seminars on the subject and devoured every piece of information I could get on the art of presenting. I was looking for a system that would help *anyone* become a powerfully persuasive speaker.

What I found is that while there is no system that will guarantee the success of your presentation, there are little-known techniques that are used by some of the world's best speakers to help win audiences over to their way of thinking.

In this book, I will reveal to you the public speaking and storytelling techniques used by four of the best speakers in the world. More specifically, you will learn how to:

- Create an opening that instantly hooks your audience into your speech.
- Keep your audience on the edge of their seats with a spellbinding story.
- Use the suspended story to keep your audience intrigued.
- Bring your characters to life.
- Turn your stories into mental movies for your audience.
- Keep ratcheting up the suspense by increasing the intensity of your conflicts.
- Create and deliver a speech your audience will remember and talk about for years.
- Add organic humor to your speeches without resorting to jokes.
- Customize your speech (and your speech) for your audience.
- Use anchors to make your points memorable.
- Use tough-watch logic to inspire your audience.
- Create a memorable and repeatable catch-phrase using "the rule of opposites".

- Create analogies and metaphors to make your message memorable.
- Add a you-focused check-in to relate with your audience.
- Give your audience dialogue to build rapport with them.
- Use Vocal variety to spice up your speech.
- Create smooth transitions to ensure your speech flows logically.
- Add credibility to your speech.
- Take an element out of your speech and put it into your audience's lives.
- Creatively summarize your main points.
- End your speech in a powerful and persuasive way.

This book is unlike most books on the subjects of public speaking and storytelling. While most books simply teach you the techniques, this book also contains short world-class speeches for you to study and evaluate. Each speech is followed by a detailed line-by-line analysis of the speech so that you can see the public speaking techniques in action.

While the four winning speeches in this book are short, inspirational speeches, the techniques in the book can be applied to create powerful business presentations, keynotes or workshops. When you apply the techniques in this book, you will become twice the speaker in half the time.

If you're ready to become a powerfully persuasive speaker who owns the stage, then let's get started...

CHAPTER TWO

THE ULTIMATE QUESTION

Speech by Lance Miller,
2005 World Champion of Public Speaking
www.LanceMillerSpeaks.com

Lance Miller is an award winning speaker and trainer. He brings to the podium a unique mix of talent and life experience that has shaped his philosophy and viewpoint of the world. He is a member of Toastmasters International and is a Distinguished Toastmaster. Lance was instrumental in building his home Toastmasters Club, Renaissance Speakers, to the #4 Toastmasters Club in the world. In 2005 he emerged from a field of 28,000 contestants from 90 countries to win the title of the World Champion of Public Speaking.

"The success of your presentation will be judged not by the knowledge you send but by what the listener receives."
Lily Walters

To get maximum value from this speech, I encourage you to watch Lance's speech. You can watch Lance in action here: *www.AkashKaria.com/Lance*

Next, read the speech transcript as it is reprinted below. As you read the speech, pay attention to the techniques Lance uses to keep his audience engaged. Jot-down your observations on a piece of paper.

Finally, read my analysis of the speech and apply the techniques to your next speech so that you too can keep your audiences mesmerized by your speeches.

Enjoy the transcript of Lance's 2005 world-championship winning speech below:

*

The Ultimate Question!

That question that has plagued man since the dawn of time.

That question that each and every one of us must ask at some point in our life.

"Do you validate?" *(audience laughter)*

I was 26 years old, I was living in a small town in Indiana,

I had a job I didn't like,

I hadn't a date in 3 years,

And I had a couple of roommates named - Mom & Dad! *(audience laughter)*

I felt like my life was going nowhere.

So I took control, I left my home and my family and moved to Los Angeles and started over!

Six months later...

I had a job I didn't like! *(audience laughter)*

I was dating a girlfriend...who trying to make me "better" by pointing out all my faults. *(audience laughter)*

And I had a couple of roommates that made Dumb and Dumber look like Einstein and Oppenhiemer. *(audience laughter)*

I had changed everything in my life - but nothing had changed.

I still felt like I was going now where.

Then one day after a business meeting, all I wanted to do was get my parking validated.

I went over the receptionist and said, "Excuse me, do you validate"

She looked up and said "Well, yes I do, you have a lovely smile.' *(audience laughter)*

Showing her the ticket I said, "I was just in a meeting with your boss, do you validate?"

And she said "Well then let me compliment you on what a fine choice of business associates you have."

I said – "You have such a keen sense of humor, I am going to go tell your boss how lucky he is to have you out here." *(audience laughter)*

She said, "Give me that that ticket!" *(audience laughter)*

She took her machine and went "Chi chink". *(Gesture of stamping the ticket)*

And then as she handed the ticket back she said, "There is something special about you."

I took the ticket and headed for the elevator, but then I stopped and turned around and just said "Thank you."

I don't how long it had been since I felt validated. Her words stayed with me all the way home. And as I was looking at my life, I started to wonder how long it had been since I validated somebody else.

I wanted to do that! I wanted to make people feel good. But I felt that I needed to be important, I needed to be successful, so that when I said something to them it would mean something.

But that receptionist had just made my day. Heck, she made my month!

With one little, "Chi chink", she stamped my ticket. And I thought – "I can do that!"

So I went home to see Dumb and Dumber. These guys were constantly bringing people back to our apartment.

It was driving me nuts! But I went in and I said, "You make friends faster than anyone I know, and that is a gift." To see their faces….I swear they got smarter right before my eyes! - "Chi chink"

I went to see my girlfriend – and I thanked her for caring enough about me to want to see me be as good as I could be. You know what? She got nicer! "Chi chink"

I went to work and I thanked my boss for hiring me. He had done me a favor, and I started enjoying my work a lot more. "Chi chink"

I used to think that I had to be important before I could validate other people. I used to look at people as obstacles to my success.

But what I discovered was that I became important when I validated someone. I became important to that person and that person.

People were the pathway to my success.

I started trying to find something I could stamp on everybody I met, that little piece of goodness, that little piece of rightness – Just a little "Chachink."

Akash Karia

I started to feel like a SUPER HERO. Underneath this mild mannered exterior was a blue and red spandex suit with a giant V on the chest. YES! I was the VALIDATOR! *(audience laughter)*

When things would get tense, they'd tighten up, I'd come in – "Chi chink", "Chi chink", "Chi chink" – I had plenty of ink! *(audience laughter)*

I'd hear people say, "Who was that man?"…"I don't know, But I heard this 'Chi chink' and I suddenly I feel so much better now!"

Then I figured it out -

Do you know what is wrong with world?

Do you know what is wrong with me?

Do you know what is wrong with you?

WHO CARES!!??? *(audience laughter)*

The question is, what is *right* with the world?

What is right with me?

What is right with you?

The common denominator of all humanity is that we are Human. We are by nature imperfect. It takes no special talent to find an imperfection in another person.

But every person goes through life wanting to be RIGHT, wanting to be VALUABLE.

Find that!

I started to discover in my life that I got what I validated. I found out that I brought out the goodness, the value others by validating that.

We have a lot of problems in this world. But I have learned that there is not a problem that exists between a parent and child, between a husband and wife, between a worker and his employer or between races, cultures or nations, that does not stem directly from an inability or an unwillingness to validate the rightness, the value and goodness in another.

This is the Ultimate Question – Do Your Validate?

But this is not what is important.

What's important is:

Can you – Chi – *(Chink)*

Can you – Chi – *(Chink)*

Can you – Chi – *(Chink)*

Oh! And one more thing: You've been a Wonderful Audience! "Chi chink!"

CHAPTER THREE

HOW TO CREATE A SPELLBINDING STORY

"It takes one hour of preparation for each minute of presentation time."
Wayne Burgraff

YOUR OPENING SHOULD CREATE QUESTIONS IN YOUR AUDIENCE'S MIND

Lance's opening creates curiosity and captures audience attention straight away because it gets audience members thinking, "What is he talking about?"

> The Ultimate Question!

> That question that has plagued man since the dawn of time.

> That question that each and every one of us must ask at some point in our life.

As soon as Lance delivers the above opening, what do you think the audience is wondering? They're wondering, "What is the Ultimate Question?"

Whenever you create questions in your audience's minds, you've got them hooked into your speech because you've aroused their curiosity.

Look at your speech opening and ask yourself, "What questions pop into my audience's minds as soon as I deliver this opening?" If your audience has no questions … you need a new opening.

INTRODUCE YOUR PROBLEM/CONFLICT EARLY ON

The hook of any story is the conflict. It's the conflict in a movie that keeps listeners glued to the screen. It's the conflict in a book that keeps readers glued to the page. And it's the conflict in your story that keeps listeners glued to your speech.

Lance introduces the problem early on in the speech. His problem was that he felt his "life was going nowhere":

> I felt like my life was going nowhere – So I took control, I left my home and my family and moved to Los Angeles and started over!
>
> 6 months later - I had a job I didn't like!
>
> I was dating a girl… who trying to make me "better" by pointing out all my faults.
>
> And I had a couple of roommates that made Dumb and Dumber look like Einstein and Oppenhiemer.

I had changed everything in my life - but nothing had changed.

I still felt like I was going now where.

In your speeches and presentations, introduce the conflict early on. The conflict captures audience attention because it gets your audience members thinking, "I wonder how this is going to end."

THE CATALYST FOR CHANGE

In my book, *Speak Like a Winner*, I analyze a speech by Darren LaCroix, the 2001 World Champion of Public Speaking. In his winning speech, *Ouch,* Darren's mentor (the "guru" in Darren's speech) gives him the following piece of wisdom:

> Rick said, "Darren, every comedian, every speaker, anyone who has accomplished anything, has fallen on their face."
> - from the speech *"Ouch"* by Darren LaCroix

In the same book, I analyze a story by Craig Valentine, the 1999 World Champion of Public Speaking.

In the story, when Craig is struggling between following his dream and continuing with his high-paying career, Craig's wife gives him the following piece of advice:

She said, "Craig...this is all you've ever talked about. This is all you've ever wanted! I don't care how much they try to compensate you...your dream is not for sale!"

- from *"Six Figure Story"* by Craig Valentine

In both Darren's and Craig's speeches, there is a guru who says something profound and wise. The guru's inspiring dialogue serves as the main message for Darren's and Craig's speeches.

However, in Lance's speech, do you notice that the main hero of the speech - the receptionist - doesn't *say* anything profound? However, the receptionist is the hero of the speech because she is the one from whom Lance learns the importance of validation.

The receptionist doesn't offer any profound wisdom or ideas, but she is a "Catalyst for Change." She is the stimulus that sparks the change in Lance's life. The inspiration comes not from what the Catalyst for Change *says*, but from what Lance *learns* from his interaction with her.

Thus, when creating your next story, you have two options:

(1) You can include a *guru* in your speech ... someone who says something profound and inspiring (such as in Craig's and Darren's speeches). The guru's words act as the stimulus that allows the main character to overcome the conflict he/she was facing.

Or

(2) You can include a Catalyst for Change in your speech ... someone who serves as the stimulus for change in the main character (such as in Lance's speech). The Catalyst for Change doesn't have to *say* anything profound, but he/she does need to impact the main character in a way that teaches the character something new. The *experience* with the Catalyst for Change can lead the main character to a new revelation. It can prove to be the spark that leads to self-examination and causes the character to learn something new, the way Lance did:

> "And as I was looking at my life, I started to wonder how long it had been since I validated somebody else."

However, whether you choose to use a Guru or a Catalyst for Change as the main hero in your speech, you do need to make *someone else* the hero of your speech.

DON'T BE THE HERO OF YOUR OWN STORY

In Craig's, Darren's and Lance's speeches, the heroes of the speeches are not the speakers. In Craig's speech, the hero is Craig's wife. In Darren's speech, Rick is the hero. And in Lance's speech, the receptionist is the hero.

So, why do you need to make someone else the hero of your story?

First, if you make yourself the hero of your story, the audience might perceive you as being arrogant. You may be perceived as a know-it-all who is simply flaunting his own achievements.

Second and more importantly, you will fail to connect with audience members if you position yourself as the hero of your own story. They will come to see you as someone who has never faced doubts and difficulties, someone who has always had all the right answers, and as a result, they will discard your advice and your message.

Finally, your speech will lack believability if you position yourself as the hero of your own story. Let's take Lance's speech as an example.

In this speech, Lance initially feels frustrated that his life is going nowhere. Now, imagine if halfway through the speech, Lance suddenly says, "And then, while driving home one night, I suddenly realized that the secret to turning my life around was to simply start validating other people!"

See, isn't that hard to believe? Audience members are probably thinking, "Wow, how did he suddenly come across that stroke of insight? And how come he'd never had it before?" By making someone else the hero of the story (whether it's the "guru" or the "catalyst for change"), your speech becomes more believable to your audience.

Who's the hero of your story?

CHOOSE ONE SOURCE TO SYMBOLIZE THE GURU/CATALYST FOR CHANGE

You're probably saying, "Akash, there are a lot of people who've influenced me and given me great advice. What if there are hundreds of sources (people, books, quotes, etc.) that could be the guru/catalyst for change in my speech?"

In this case, choose *one* person or book or quote that can represent all the hundreds of sources that have influenced you. Simply distill all the advice that you've learned from hundreds of books and people and make one source the guru/catalyst for change.

For example, in Lance's speech, I'm pretty sure that Lance learned about validating other people from lots of sources. He probably learned about the importance of validating other people from books he's read, teachers he's had, friends he hangs around with, etc. However, the receptionist is the main hero of the story and represents all these other sources that have influenced Lance.

If you have multiple sources that could serve as a guru/catalyst for change, simply choose one source that can represent the advice and wisdom you received from all the others.

LOOK FOR HUMOR OPPORTUNITIES WITHIN DIALOGUE

Lance's speech is a very humorous one. The best speeches get the audience members to laugh and learn at the same time.

Humor doesn't mean having to steal jokes from the Internet. I recommend against using jokes from the Internet for several reasons:

- Jokes off the Internet are not usually funny.

- The ones that are funny are usually well known. Your audience members are likely to know the joke, which means that they know the punch line. If they know the punch line, the joke lacks the element of surprise (the sudden twist) and hence won't produce a laugh.

- Jokes subtract from your credibility. If audience members have heard the joke before, they'll label you as unoriginal. This negative perception will be hard to break.

- Jokes usually detract from your message. They usually are not related to your speech and take away from your main message. Audience members hate listening to jokes that have nothing to do with the speech.

So, how do you add humor to your speech if you shouldn't use jokes?

Look for humor opportunities within dialogue (hat tip: Craig Valentine).

Whenever you have an exchange of dialogue between characters, look for humor opportunities. What witty remark can a character make? What humorous line of dialogue can you add?

Let's have a look at examples of humor within dialogue in Lance's speech:

> I went over the receptionist and said, "Excuse me, do you validate?"
>
> She looked up and said "Well yes I do, you have a lovely smile." (audience laughter)

Now, here's the secret to humor: **A comment is humorous when it sets up an expectation, and then breaks it.**

Lance's line *("Excuse me, do you validate?")* sets up an expectation that the next answer will be a "Yes" or a "No," but the receptionist's line (*"Well, yes I do, you have a lovely smile."*) breaks the expectation and hence causes audience members to laugh.

Furthermore, this is great wordplay. The word validate has two meanings. The first meaning refers to "authenticate" a parking ticket. The second meaning refers to making people feel good about themselves. Lance's line refers to the first meaning (about parking), setting up the expectation that the receptionist's reply should be about the parking ticket. However, the receptionist's reply breaks the expectation by referring to the second meaning. Can you use wordplay to add humor to your speeches?

Okay, let's get back to examining humor within dialogue. Here's another example from Lance's speech:

> I said – "You have such a keen sense of humor, I am going to go tell your boss how lucky he is to have you out here." (audience laughter)

> She said, "Give me that that ticket!" (audience laughter)

Can you see how the witty interaction between Lance and the receptionist adds humor to the speech?

Whenever you have two characters interacting with each other, put yourself in the characters' shoes. Imagine yourself as the characters as you hear the dialogue flowing back and forth. While in character, try to come up with witty remarks for the characters to say to each other.

This technique is difficult to use because it requires you to think creatively. However, the more you do it, the easier it becomes to spot humor opportunities within dialogue.

To practice this technique, I encourage you to apply it in your daily conversations. When you're hanging out with your friends and family, try to respond to some of their comments with witty remarks. The more you make your friends and family laugh, the better you'll become at creating witty conversations between characters in your speeches.

LOOK FOR STORIES IN YOUR EVERYDAY LIFE

"Your life tells a story and there is someone out there who needs to hear it. You may think your story is not sensational, but it does not have to be sensational. It just has to be sincere. If your audience can relate to you and your experiences, and chances are they will, then you need to tell them what you have been through, share your life, share your love and share your message with the world."
~ Mark Brown,
1995 World Champion of Public Speaking

I once had a newbie speaker approach me after a Toastmasters conference and say, "Akash, I don't really know what to talk about in my next speech. I've never had any dramatic experiences in my life, so I don't have any exciting stories. What should I do if I don't have any life-or-death type of stories to share with my audience?"

You don't need to tell dramatic stories about life-or-death scenarios in order to have a great speech. Instead, look for the stories in your everyday life. Which stories do you most often entertain your friends with? Which stories do you share with your family at the dinner table?

Once you've discovered these stories from your everyday life, ask yourself, "What lesson can I learn from this story?"

Sure, audience members are motivated by dramatic stories such as a rags-to-riches story or a story of how a woman went from being a depressed, lonely alcoholic to being a happily married, sober mother of four. These stories are motivating and dramatic, but your audience members can connect just as much with smaller (non-dramatic) achievements.

They will connect with how you went from being slightly overweight to losing a couple of pounds.

They'll connect with how you went from struggling with credit card debt to being debt free.

They'll connect with the story of how you went from always hitting snooze on your alarm to waking up early and being on time for work.

Why will your audience members connect with these smaller, non-dramatic achievements? Because your audience members can relate to the struggles of being slightly overweight, being in debt and waking up late. These are issues that most of your audience members can empathize with and may even be going through. Sharing these stories will help you connect with your audience.

So stop worrying about not having a dramatic enough message or an inspiring enough story. Share stories about common everyday worries and stresses, and you'll connect with your audience.

By the way, Lance's regional winning speech (the one that helped him win a spot in the World Championship of Public Speaking finals) was about his struggles trying to lose a couple of pounds, pay off his credit card debt and wake up on time! The audience loved his speech. In fact, that simple speech is one of my favorite speeches.

As Lance's speeches show, your stories don't need to be dramatic incidents from your life. In *The Ultimate Question*, Lance tells a simple story about a cheeky receptionist who taught him an important lesson.

Most average speakers would toss out this kind of story, thinking that it wasn't dramatic enough. Masterful speakers realize that great stories don't need to be dramatic: they can be everyday stories that can both entertain and educate your audience.

PROVIDE THE RESOLUTION

In any story, there should be a resolution to the conflict. In this speech, the resolution is that as soon as Lance begins to validate the people around him, his life gets better:

> I went to see my girlfriend – "And I thanked her for caring enough about me to want to see me be as good as I could be." You know what - She got nicer! "Chi chink"

I went to work and I thanked my boss for hiring me, he had done me a favor, and I started enjoying my work a lot more. "Chi chink"

What's the resolution to the conflict in your speech?

REPEAT YOUR CATCH PHRASE OFTEN

Most great speeches repeat a catch phrase several times throughout the speech so that audience members will remember the main message of the speech.

In Martin Luther King's iconic speech, the catch phrase was "I have a dream," which he repeated nine times throughout the speech.

The catch phrase in Barack Obama's 2008 speech was "Yes, we can!"

In Darren LaCroix's speech, the catch phrase was "Ouch!"

In Lance's speech, the catch phrase is the "Chichink" sound effect, which represents the act of validating people. Every time he says "Chichink," he reinforces his message and ensures that it will be remembered.

As these speeches show, you can use a phrase, a word or even a sound effect as a catch phrase.

Having a catch phrase will make your message memorable. The audience will remember your catch phrase, and thus they'll remember your message.

SHOW THE CHANGE IN CHARACTER

In a good story, the protagonist in the story must change as a result of the wisdom of the guru.

In this speech, you can see the change in Lance's character as Lance begins to validate the people around him:

Before the Catalyst for Change:

> I had a job I didn't like,
>
> I was dating a girlfriend... who trying to make me "better" by pointing out all my faults.
>
> And I had a couple of roommates that made Dumb and Dumber look like Einstein and Oppenhiemer.

After the Catalyst for Change:

> But I went in and I said, "You make friends faster than anyone I know, and that is a gift." To see their faces....I swear they got smarter right before my eyes! - "Chi chink"
>
> I went to see my girlfriend – "And I thanked her for caring enough about me to want to see me be as good as I could be." You know what - She got nicer! "Chi chink"
>
> I went to work and I thanked my boss for hiring me, he had done me a favor, and I started enjoying my work a lot more. "Chi chink"

In addition to experiencing more harmony with his roommates, enjoying his job more and having a nicer girlfriend, Lance's attitude changes from seeing people as "obstacles" to seeing them as "pathways to success":

> I used to think that I had to be important before I could validate other people. I used to look at people as obstacles s to my success.

> But what I discovered was that I became important when I validated someone. I became important to that person and that person.

> People were the pathway to my success.

What changes occur in your main character's life and attitude as a result of having overcome the conflict?

YOUR STORY DOESN'T HAVE TO MAKE PEOPLE CRY!

One of the mistakes I first made when I started speaking competitively was that I thought great speeches needed to make people cry. Many other speakers make this same mistake. Thus, when choosing topics for competitive speeches, they (like me) *only* focus on topics such as the death of a loved one, battles with cancer, etc.

While there's nothing wrong with talking about such emotional topics, it's important to realize that your speeches don't *necessarily* have to make people cry. As Lance's winning speech shows, a winning speech doesn't have to make the audience cry. It can still be a winning speech if it makes the audience *laugh* and *learn*.

As long as you touch the audience's emotion in some way (whether it's making them cry or making them laugh – or both), you can create a winning speech using any topic that you feel strongly about and which has a message that is relevant to your audience.

END WITH AUDIENCE PARTICIPATION

The beginning and the end are the most important parts of your speech because audience members remember the first and the last thing they hear.

Thus, if you end your speech poorly, your audience will leave thinking, "That really was quite a disappointing ending and a disappointing speech!"

If, however, you end your speech in a memorable manner that excites your audience members, they'll leave raving about your speech.

Since the ending of the speech is so important to the success of your presentation, I advise you to spend time working on your closing.

Lance ends his speech masterfully. What does he do that's so great? He ends his speech with audience participation. At the end of the speech, when he says "Can you Chi-," the audience finishes the phrase with "chink":

Can you – Chi – *audience says*: "Chink"

Can you – Chi – *audience says*: "Chink"

Can you – Chi – *audience says*: "Chink"

Why is ending with audience participation such a great strategy?

First, by getting your audience members physically involved in your speech, you raise the energy level in the room. Thus, when your audience members walk out of your speech, they'll remember your speech as being energetic, exciting and interactive! In other words, they'll think it was a great speech.

More importantly, getting your audience members to repeat your key phrase back to you ensures that it will be remembered. If they say your key phrase, they will retain it longer than if you simply told it to them. Think about it: Isn't it true that you're more likely to remember something you said than something someone told you?

You're probably thinking, "Akash, isn't ending with audience participation an incredibly risky strategy?" The answer is...yes, trying to end with audience participation is a riskier strategy than simply ending with a summary of your message.

What are the risks? Well, for one, the audience might not be willing to participate. For example, I once saw a speaker (let's call her Judy) whose call for audience participation was met by awkward silence. Judy asked us - her audience - to repeat her key phrase with her, but she was met with silence because:

(1)   She hadn't repeated her key phrase often enough. Hence, we didn't know what her key phrase was! How could we repeat her key phrase when we didn't know what it was?

(2)   Her key phrase was too long to memorize. Her key phrase was so long I wasn't even able to count the number of words in it!

How can you avoid encountering such an embarrassing situation?

Simply, there are three things you can do.

First, keep your key phrase shorter than seven words to make sure that it's short enough to be remembered. According to research, most people can only remember seven units of information.

Next, repeat your key phrase several times throughout your speech. Make sure your audience has been exposed to your key phrase enough times to have a chance to remember it.

Finally, and most importantly, make sure you practice in front of a live audience before you deliver your speech. If Judy had practiced her speech in front of a live audience, she would have realized that her audience participation strategy wasn't working. She then could have made appropriate changes to her speech, helping her avoid the embarrassing situation of being met by silence on stage.

Anyway, at least Judy learned an important lesson.

And now you know that lesson too, so make sure that you practice your speech at least once in front of a live audience! You could save yourself some very embarrassing moments.

Plus, you'll get valuable feedback about how to make your speech even better.

SPEAKING TOOLKIT SUMMARY #1
ACTIONABLE KNOWLEDGE

"They may forget what you said,
but they will never forget how you made them feel."
Carl W. Buechner

- Create an opening that creates curiosity.
- Introduce the problem/conflict early on.
- Your speech doesn't *have* to make audience members cry.
- Get your audience members to laugh and learn at the same time.
- Uncover humor from dialogue.
- Make someone else the hero of your story.
- Introduce a Guru/Catalyst for Change.
- Look for stories in your everyday life.
- Provide a resolution to the conflict.
- Characters must change as a result of the conflict.
- Your story doesn't have to make your audience cry.
- Create a catch phrase.
- Practice in front of a live audience at least once.
- Repeat your key phrase often.
- Keep your key phrase short.
- End with audience participation.

CHAPTER FOUR

FINDING YOUR RHTHYM

Speech by Loghandran Krishnasamy
First Runner Up – 2008 World Championship
of Public Speaking

Loghandran Krishnasamy is a corporate financial training consultant, actor and stand-up comedian who was the First Runner-Up in the 2008 World Championship of Public Speaking.

"The success of your presentation will be judged not by the knowledge you send but by what the listener receives."
Lily Walters

To get maximum value from this speech, I encourage you to watch Loghandran's speech here:
www.AkashKaria.com/Krishnasamy

Next, read the speech transcript as it is reprinted on the next page.

As you read the speech, pay attention to the techniques Loghandran uses to keep his audience captivated.

Enjoy the speech (below):

*

When my boss announced that he was going to retire, he called me into the room and told me this: "I've got one million in the retirement fund. I do not have any financial obligations, my two daughters are happily married, I don't have any problems with my wife…but, I am not happy! You are the hotshot Toastmaster, you tell me *why?*" *(Facial expression to show being dumb)*

I wondered, "Did I miss out any manual on happiness by Toastmasters?" *(audience laughter)*

I had to answer him, so I said, "Boss, you have achieved whatever you want in life. You've got everything you want. You don't have to achieve anything else. You have reached a plateau in your life. Hah, that's why!" *(Delivery in a submissive manner to boss)*

He was not happy with my answer. *(audience laughter)*

Neither was I.

This question has been haunting me for quite some time, and I have been searching for the answer.

Come, join me in this search.

I need your help on this one.

Take your two fingers on your right hand…put it on your pulse…amplify the sound for me by snapping your fingers. *(audience involvement)*

Thank you!

You have found the rhythm that puts a dance in your step, and takes you to the dance-floor of life.

The rhythm is everywhere.

I was once assigned to take twelve blind children to the park. Now, that is a logistical *nightmare! (audience laughter)*

I told them, "What if you fall into the lake and the monster comes and eats you up?"

They said, "We will *fight* the monster!" *(Imitating a child's voice)*

So I decided to take them to the park. The moment they went to the park, they were all in excitement!

What excited them?

So I closed my eyes…to see what they were seeing.

The sun's rays came through the trees and formed little rays of light that formed a kaleidoscope of colors that excited them.

And one girl hugged a tree and said, "I can see God!" *(audience laughter)*

Apparently, the tiny nodes in the bark of the tree had four dots, three dots and three dots in configurations that were in the Braille alphabet that spelled GOD.

And in rained! Suddenly, they were all in excitement. Their music? The rhythm of the falling rain…pitter-patter on their delicate skins.

When the blind find their rhythm, they are in a presence. They are in the dance of the divine! They can find rhythm to life.

The rhythm can also be found at any age. I have a neighbor who is seventy-five years old and he's always telling me to take up Tai Chi *(demonstration)*

I told him, "As a manager in the office, I'm already doing it. I take work from this side and give it this side! It's called delegation." *(audience laughter)*

He said, "No no no no. Tai Chi is for blood circulation. See my palms? You will see flushed with red!"

I told him, "With the kind of creditors after me, my blood circulates automatically! My face is always red." *(audience laughter)*

Then he said, "You must take Tai Chi because at seventy-five, you should be able to tie your shoe-lace standing on one-foot!" *(Display the stance without moving)*

Show-off! *(audience laughter)*

Only later did I realize that he had an artificial left foot.

Mr. Lim was able to find rhythm even in a docile exercise like Tai Chi.

If you do not find your rhythm, it may be too late.

In my country, Malaysia, the penalty for murder is hanging till death. And 90% of the accused will plead with their lawyers to ask for a life-sentence instead of facing death. They know that when death knocks, they have wasted life. They prefer a life-sentence in prison rather than a rhythm stopped. *(Pause)*

My friends, remember this. Life does not owe you an answer! You have to find *your* rhythm.

If the blind can find their rhythm, and if the aged their rhythm...you can also do it.

When death knocks on your door, open it. Get dressed up. Put on your best shoes and say, "I had the dance of my life!"

Till we meet again, in the distant shores...

CHAPTER FIVE

HOW TO INSPIRE AND IMPACT YOUR AUDIENCE

"There are three things to aim at in public speaking: first, to get into your subject, then to get your subject into yourself, and lastly, to get your subject into the heart of your audience."
Alexander Gregg

WHAT'S THE QUESTION THAT NEEDS ANSWERING/ PROBLEM THAT NEEDS SOLVING?

In Loghandran's speech, the question that needs answering is, "Why is it that a person who has everything is unhappy?"

What's the question in your speech that needs answering?

Write out the question in less than 20 words. If it takes you more than 20 words to summarize the main question of your speech, then your question is not clear enough.

Once you've discovered and written down the main question of your speech, come up with examples, analogies and stories to answer the question.

When you present your audience members with a question to answer or a problem to solve, their minds unconsciously become obsessed with trying to figure out the answer/the solution.

POSE THE PROBLEM IMMEDIATELY

Loghandran dives into a story about his boss calling him into the office and immediately presents the problem that needs to be solved:

> "I've got one million in the retirement fund. I do not have any financial obligations, my two daughters are happily married, I don't have any problems with my wife…but, I am not happy! You are the hotshot Toastmaster, you tell me why?"

(Side note by Loghandran: "Hot shot" is American conversational English. Choose conversational words over the perfect adjective.)

By presenting the problem that needs solving, Loghandran hooks his audience into his speech because his audience begins to think, "Interesting. Why is it that a rich man who has everything would not be happy?"

In your speeches and presentations, present the problem immediately. If it's a problem that audience members can relate to, you'll immediately have their full attention.

POSE THE PROBLEM IN THE FORM OF A STORY

An average speaker might choose to start off this speech with something along the lines of:

> "I know many people have everything they need. They have millions of dollars in the retirement fund and they have no financial obligations. Yet, most of these people are unhappy. Why is this so?"

That's a *good* opening, but not a *great* one. It's good because it captures audience attention with a question and gets people's minds working. However, this good opening could become a *great* opening if it was presented in the form of a <u>story</u>.

(Side note by Loghandran: This is a very important point. At the 2012 semifinal speech contest, I can easily detect 32 speakers making this mistake.)

Notice how Loghandran presents the problem using a story. Instead of generalizing, Loghandran uses his boss's story to pose the question that needs answering. Using the story, Loghandran offers a *concrete example* of someone who has it all but it isn't happy. This concrete example gives the speech extra credibility because it's *proof* that there are people who have no financial obligations and yet they are not happy.

(Side note by Loghandran: When you generalize, your words are bound to be heard as clichéd. But if you are specific, as in the boss example, the words are fresh.)

In your speech, consider presenting the problem in the form of a story.

CUSTOMIZE YOUR HUMOR FOR YOUR AUDIENCE

Loghandran is talking to a Toastmasters audience, so his humor is tailor-made for them:

> I wondered, "Did I miss out any manual on happiness by Toastmasters?"

People outside the Toastmasters organization won't laugh at the above line. However, the line works perfectly for the Toastmasters audience.

When creating your speech, study your audience. Which organization do they belong to? What activities do they do that no one else does? What makes them unique?

By studying your audience, you will discover new humor opportunities. In addition, learning about your audience will allow you to use the information you learn to create not just customized humor, but also a speech that **resonates** well with that particular audience.

USE AN ACTIVITY TO ANCHOR YOUR POINT

There are four types of anchors you can use to hook your point to your listeners' memories. Anchors are tools you can use to make your point stick to your listeners' long-term memory.

I learned the four anchors from Craig Valentine's superb book, *World Class Speaking:*

- **Anecdote**: An anecdote is a story. Stories are memorable, and when people remember your story, they remember the point associated with it. For example, have you heard the story of the boy who cried wolf? Even if you heard this story when you were a young child, you probably still remember the story and the point associated with it. That's the power of a well-told story: it sticks.

- **Acronym**: An acronym is a memory tool. For example, if I was giving a speech, I might use the acronym "BEST," where the letter B would stand for something, E would stand for something else, S would represent the third point and T would represent the final point in my speech.

(Side note by Loghandran: I would not encourage use of acronyms. The danger of using acronyms is: A) The speech will look clichéd. B) The speech will look instructional. People like to learn but they do not like to be taught. The audience should learn from the story and should not be taught a lesson from the speaker.)

(Side note by Akash: I agree that acronyms may not work too well for an inspirational speech. However, for an instructional speech, an acronym may be a great choice).

- **Analogy:** An analogy helps make a point clearer, and it makes the point memorable. For example, in *Ouch*, his world championship speech, Darren LaCroix uses the analogy of comparing failure to falling on your face.

- **Activity:** The final anchor is an activity. If you can create an activity that backs up your point, then your point will be remembered.

In this speech, Loghandran uses an activity to make his point memorable:

I need your help on this one.

Take your two fingers on your right hand…put it on your pulse…amplify the sound for me by snapping your fingers.

Thank you!

You have found the rhythm that puts a dance in your step, and takes you to the dance-floor of life.

The snapping of fingers with 2,000 people in the room makes the point memorable. In addition, the audience participation helps Loghandran's speech stand out from the rest of the competition.

In your speeches and presentations, make sure you tie every point to an anchor to make your point memorable.

USE BEAUTIFUL, VIVID DESCRIPTIONS

Loghandran uses beautiful and vivid descriptions that make the scenes come alive. Consider the following descriptions:

> "The sun's rays came through the trees and formed little rays of light that formed a kaleidoscope of colors"

> "Their music? The rhythm of the falling rain...pitter patter on their delicate skins."

Notice that the description is beautiful, yet it is not overly poetic. Overly poetic, long-winded descriptions can slow down a story and bore an audience. Save the poetic descriptions for a novel.

In your speeches, aim for beautiful, vivid descriptions that make the scene come alive without slowing down the story.

MAKE A POINT, TELL A STORY

Loghandran uses a very simple, yet effective speech structure. He makes a point, and then follows it up with a story.

In this speech, Loghandran makes two main points. First, he says, "The rhythm is everywhere," and then follows the statement with a story about blind children finding their rhythm. (Side note by Loghandran: "The rhythm is everywhere" is also a transition to the story.)

Next, Loghandran makes the point that "The rhythm can be found at any age" and follows that with a humorous story about Mr. Lim. (Side note by Loghandran: "The rhythm can be found at any age" is also a transition.)

Make a Point, Tell a Story: It's a simple yet proven-to-work speech structure. Use it!

TOUGH WATCH LOGIC

In his book, "*Winning Arguments: Everything You Need to Know About the Art of Persuasion,*" Jay Heinreich explains "tough watch logic." Here's my explanation:

Have you ever seen the advertisement for a watch that manages to keep on ticking even under extreme conditions? For example, the ad shows the following scenes: the watch continues ticking even when it's 20,000 miles underwater; it's run over by a monster truck but emerges without a scratch.

Can you picture the type of ad I'm talking about?

Well, tough-watch logic is when audience members think, "If the watch works under such tough conditions, I definitely shouldn't have a problem with it in my everyday life."

In this speech, Loghandran uses a similar form of "tough watch logic." He shows that blind children can find their rhythm and even 75-year-olds can find their rhythm. Using such extreme examples causes audience members to think, "If they can find their rhythm, then I can too!"

INSPIRE PEOPLE BY TALKING ABOUT PEOPLE WHO INSPIRE YOU

In many speeches, the inspirational person is ultimately the speaker.

For example, in my first book, *Speak Like a Winner*, I feature a speech by Craig Valentine, the 1999 World Champion of Public Speaking. Craig Valentine's speech, we are inspired by his example to follow his dream.

In the same book, I feature a speech by Darren LaCroix, the 2001 World Champion of Public Speaking. In Darren LaCroix's speech, we are inspired by how Darren overcomes his failures and ultimately achieves success.

The afore-mentioned examples are great speeches. However, your speeches don't necessarily have to have you - the speaker - as the inspirational character. The other option is to talk about people in your life who inspire you.

For example, in this speech, Loghandran is not the inspirational character in the story. Instead, the inspirational characters are the blind children and Mr. Lim.

Warning: While it is okay to talk about inspirational people such as Dr. Martin Luther King, Nelson Mandela and Abraham Lincoln, I recommend against this because most of your audience members are already familiar with these stories. As a result, they have no reason to listen because they're not receiving any new information. (Side note by Loghandran: There is also the danger of being clichéd. Therefore not fresh and thus boring.)

If you're going to give an inspirational speech about someone else, it's best to give a speech about an inspirational character you know personally. This has two advantages:

First, because you know this character personally, your speech has high credibility because you're telling a story where you have first-hand knowledge about the experiences someone went through.

Secondly, audience members most likely won't know the story of the person you're talking about, so they have a reason to listen because they are receiving a new and valuable story.

END WITH THE KEY TAKEAWAY FOR THE AUDIENCE

End your speech with the key takeaway message for the audience. In Loghandran's speech, the key takeaway is:

> You have to find your rhythm.
>
> If the blind can find their rhythm, and if the aged their rhythm…you can also do it.
>
> When death knocks on your door, open it. Get dressed up. Put on your best shoes and say, "I had the dance of my life!"

What is it that you want the audience to do, think or feel because of having listened to your speech? Make sure that this comes across clearly in your conclusion.

SPEAKING TOOLKIT SUMMARY #2
ACTIONABLE KNOWLEDGE

"Put the argument into a concrete shape, into an image, some hard phrase, round and solid as a ball, which they can see and handle and carry home with them, and the cause is half won."
Ralph Waldo Emerson

- Pose the problem immediately
- Pose the problem as a story
- What's the question that needs answering?
- Customize your humor (and your speech) through audience analysis
- Use an activity to anchor your point (4A's of anchors)
- Create beautiful, vivid descriptions
- Use "tough watch" logic
- Talk about people who've inspired you
- End with your key takeaway message

CHAPTER SIX

IT'S NOT ABOUT THE KNOCKDOWN

Speech by Ian Humphrey
Finalist – 2010 World Championship of Public Speaking
www.BeIanSpired.com

Ian Humphrey is a dynamic youth speaker who placed as one of the top nine speakers in the world out of 30,000 competitors in the 2010 World Championship of Public Speaking.

"The success of your presentation will be judged not by the knowledge you send but by what the listener receives."
Lily Walters

You know the drill by now. First, watch a short clip Ian's speech: *www.AkashKaria.com/Ian*

Next, read the speech transcript as it is reprinted and pay attention to the techniques Ian uses to keep his audience hooked onto his every word. Enjoy the speech:

*

BOOM! Down Goes Muhammad Ali!

February 10th 1962, professional boxer Muhammad Ali was knocked down for the first time in his *life*, by Sonny Banks. As the referee began his count to ten, Ali says that he sat up, looked around and thought to himself, *"The canvas is no place for a champion."*

So he rose to his feet, dusted himself off….made sure he was still pretty…then he hit Sonny Banks so hard, Mrs. Banks got a headache! *(audience laughter)*

Mr. Contest chair, fellow toastmasters and guests. On that day, Muhammad Ali proved to the world, but more importantly to himself, that it's not about the *knockdown*, it's about the getup. It's about what we do after the knockdown, that is what defines *who-we- are*.

Now I'm not a boxer. I've had three fights in my life…and my sister won all three. *(audience laughter)*

Boxer or not, I believe I can say at some point we all get hit on the blindside. KNOCKED upside the head, POW, by life*!*

I guess you could say life at times will be your Sonny Banks, knocking you down flat on your back, then taunting you with a question like, *"What are you gonna do now?"*

Like you, I've faced my Sonny Banks many times. He began throwing punches at me long before I had taken my first breath.

You see, I was born two months premature after my mom was assaulted by a neighbor. I remained in the hospital for months, my family unsure when I'd be allowed to go home. Three years later, I found and swallowed a bottle of prescription medication that put me in a coma doctors did not believe I'd survive. Because of that incident my mom lost custody of me and I was placed in a foster home. While in that home, I was locked inside a closet, mentally and physically abused. BUT I WAS STILL STANDING!

At the age of eleven, I held on to the hope of knowing my mom was about to regain custody of me, but before that could happen, she passed away. BOOM! That was the knockdown blow for me. I went down and I stayed down. I stayed down and allowed life to begin to count me out.

ONE!

I gave up and started feeling sorry for myself!

TWO!

I surrounded myself with all of the wrong people!

THREE, FOUR!

Their bad habits quickly became my bad habits.

FIVE, SIX!

At the age of nineteen, I was sentenced to fifteen years in prison!

SEVEN, EIGHT!

Ashamed of the person I had allowed myself to become, I finally began to plead for help.

NINE!

A prison councilor named Charles Lyles saw something in me that I didn't know was there and said, "Young man, this doesn't have to be your life. You are capable of doing great things."

Before walking away, he looked at me and said, "*I believe in you.*"

That was the first time I had ever heard those words!

That's when I got up. I got up by repeating his words to myself over and over again.

"Someone believes in you. You can do great things."

Soon his words became my words and I began to believe in myself.

I GOT UP, by refusing to continue feeling sorry for myself. I GOT UP, by looking for the lesson behind the knockdown. I GOT UP, BY FOCUSING ON MY future instead of my past.

Now I'm sure you're all thinking, "I bet after he got up, his Sonny Banks left him alone and he's lived happily ever after. As my children would say…"NOT"

We all know life doesn't work that way. My Sonny Banks continues to follow me around trying to knock me back down.

And you know what? Sometimes he succeeds. But I get up, I brush myself off and move forward.

When did you get up?

Or have you?

Perhaps you're preparing to fight some of life's toughest opponents, or maybe your back is already on the canvas.

I don't believe it matters where you ARE, as long as you know there have been others that have faced those same opponents and won, then you have to know that it's *POSSIBLE* that you too *can win*!

On that day in 1962 everyone that witnessed that fight, knew Muhammad Ali was down, but only he knew that he wasn't out.

The next time life knocks you down the most important thing you can do is find a way to *rise*.

Because it's not about the knockdown, it's about the getup.

It's what you do *after* the knockdown that is what *defines* who you *are*!

CHAPTER SEVEN

HOW TO TURN YOUR STORY INTO A LIFE-CHANGING SPEECH

"What is conceived well is expressed clearly."
Nicolas Boileau-Despréaux

BEGIN WITH A BOOM!

Ian starts off in the middle of the action, with Muhammad Ali being knocked down. Starting off in the middle of the action grabs audience attention straight away:

BOOM! Down Goes Muhammad Ali!

This opening is similar to an action movie that grabs your attention by starting off in the middle of a high-speed car chase.

In your speech, dive straight into the most exciting part of your story. Throw your audience members straight into the most exciting scene and they will have no choice but to be wrapped up in your story.

USE ANOTHER PERSON'S STORY AS AN EXAMPLE TO BACK UP YOUR POINT

Ian uses Muhammad's Ali's knockdown story to prove his point.

> On that day, Muhammad Ali proved to the world, but more importantly to himself, that it's not about the knockdown, it's about the getup.

You can use a short third-person story in your story as an example to prove your point.

Whose story will you use as an example?

USE AN ANALOGY/METAPHOR

Muhammad Ali's knockdown story is a perfect lead-in for using boxing as a metaphor for life. Ian takes the element of being knocked down in boxing and applies it to audience members' lives by comparing being knocked down in boxing to being knocked down by life's challenges:

> Boxer or not, I believe I can say at some point we all get hit on the blindside. KNOCKED upside the head, POW, by life!

A metaphor will help make abstract concepts concrete and will serve as a useful memory tool to help your audience remember your message. What element can you take out of your speech and apply to your audience members' lives?

You can also take characters out of your speech and apply them to your audience members' lives. For example, Ian applies the character of Sonny Banks to audience members' lives in such a way that Sonny Banks comes to represent all of life's toughest obstacles:

> I guess you could say life at times will be your Sonny Banks, knocking you down flat on your back, then taunting you with a question like, "What are you gonna do now?"

Later in the speech:

> Now I'm sure you're all thinking, "I bet after he got up, his Sonny Banks left him alone and he's lived happily ever after"

Each audience member has his/her own "Sonny Banks," so the strategy of taking a character out of your speech and making him/her a symbol for something in your audience's lives helps make your speech relevant to your audience. It helps you build a deeper connection with your audience because you are directly connecting to them and their issues.

Just to exhaust this point (and it is an important one), here's another example of how you can take an element out of your speech and apply it to your audience.

I recently heard a speaker talk about his incredible adventure of climbing Mount Kilimanjaro in Tanzania.

After describing the physical hardships that he went through when climbing Mount Kilimanjaro, the speaker asked us:

What mountain are you trying to climb?

Do you see how the speaker took the element of the mountain out of his speech and applied it to his audience's lives?

We may not be interested in climbing Mount Kilimanjaro, but we are interested in conquering our own personal mountain, whatever it may be.

What element can you take out of your speech and apply to your audience members' lives? This element will serve as the metaphor that you can keep calling back to throughout your speech to help deepen the connection with your audience.

GIVE YOUR AUDIENCE A LINE OF DIALOGUE/ VERBALIZE WHAT THEY ARE THINKING

You can strengthen the connection your audience feels with you by giving them dialogue.

For example, Ian gives his audience dialogue when he says:

> Now I'm sure you're all thinking, "I bet after he got up, his Sonny Banks left him alone and he's lived happily ever after."

In one of my speeches, I give my audience dialogue by saying to them:

You're probably thinking, "Akash, why's a handsome guy like you still single?" (Audience laughter)

When you know what the audience will be thinking, you can give them dialogue and address the question or thought they might be having.

Verbalizing what the audience is thinking by giving them a line of dialogue can help your audience feel like they're a part of your speech. It can also create new humor opportunities.

USE THE SINGULAR FOCUS TO HAVE A ONE-ON-ONE CONVERSATION WITH YOUR AUDIENCE

If you make your audience feel like you're talking directly to them, you'll generate such a massive level of rapport with them that they won't want your speech to finish.

So, how do you replicate the intimacy/feel of a one-on-one conversation in a speech in front of hundreds of people?

Here's a technique I learned from Craig Valentine, the 1999 World Champion of Public Speaking: Use the singular focus when speaking to your audience.

Instead of saying, "I'd like to thank you all for coming today," say "I'd like to thank *you*..."

In this speech, Ian could achieve this one-on-one connection by changing the phrase "Now I'm sure you're <u>all</u> thinking…" to "Now, *you're* thinking…"

It's a very small change to Ian's speech, but it's an effective technique. When applied throughout your speech, it can help you build an unbreakable connection with your audience.

LINK YOUR MESSAGE BACK TO YOUR LISTENERS

Ian links his message about getting up back to his audience to make sure that his speech is still relevant to them.

> When did you get up?
>
> Or have you?
>
> Perhaps you're preparing to fight some of life's toughest opponents, or maybe your back is already on the canvas.

Always make sure you link your story back to your listeners to keep them involved in your speech.

CIRCULAR CLOSING: LINK YOUR CLOSING BACK TO YOUR BEGINNING

Ian has a wonderfully circular closing. He links his closing back to the beginning of his speech:

Beginning of Ian's speech:

Down Goes Muhammad Ali…

On that day, Muhammad Ali proved to the world, but more importantly to himself, that it's not about the knockdown, it's about the getup. It's about what we do after the knockdown, that is what defines who-we- are.

Ending of Ian's speech:

On that day in 1962 everyone that witnessed that fight, knew Muhammad Ali was down, but only he knew that he wasn't out…

Because it's not about the knockdown, it's about the getup. It's what you do after the knockdown, that is what defines who you are!

Sandwiched in between the beginning and ending is Ian's personal story. This great structure makes Ian's audience members feel they have just ridden a full 360-degree emotional roller coaster of a speech.

END WITH YOUR KEY TAKEAWAY MESSAGE

The takeaway message is the main message that you want your audience to remember.

When you end with the takeaway message, you ensure that it will stick because the ending of your speech is one of the most memorable parts of your speech.

Ian ends his speech with a clear, succinct takeaway message.

What's the takeaway message of *your* speech?

ACTIONABLE KNOWLEDGE

"To be a person is to have a story to tell."
Isak Dinesen

- Begin with a BOOM!
- Use another person's story as an example to back up your main point
- Create a catch-phrase using opposites
- Use an analogy/metaphor to make your message memorable
- Add a you-focused check-in to relate with your audience
- Give your audience dialogue
- Look to one, speak to all
- Link your message back to your listeners
- Link your closing back to your opening
- End with your key takeaway message

CHAPTER EIGHT

FEED THE RIGHT DOG

Speech by Erick Rainey
2X Third Place Finalist at the World Championships of
Public Speaking (2005 & 2009)
3X Great Britain and Ireland Public Speaking Champion
www.RainWorks.co.uk

Erick Rainey is an internationally renowned public speaker, twice crowned Speech Making Champion of the UK and Ireland. He was also twice crowned 2nd Runner-Up at the World Championship of Public Speaking.

"A speech is poetry: cadence, rhythm, imagery, sweep! A speech reminds us that words, like children, have the power to make dance the dullest beanbag of a heart."
Peggy Noonan

Watch a short clip Erick's speech
(*www.AkashKaria.com/Rainey*) and then read the speech text
on the next page:

*

Shh, do you hear that?

It's a dog growling.

And another one...panting.

I recognize these sounds because...I'm a dog owner. I have two...and they're *very* hungry and they *demand* my attention!

You're a dog owner, and you're a dog owner. *(Gesture pointing to specific members of the audience)*

In fact, everyone is in this room is a dog owner...you just don't know it yet. *(audience laughter)*

I'm going to tell you about my dogs, and then I'm going to introduce *you* to yours.

Oh, they're not real...they live...up here *(gesture pointing to the head)*

I first got an inkling that there was something going on up here (gesture tapping index finger to side of head) when I was seven years old.

I was visiting my relatives in Tennessee. I walked into my cousin Will's room. There were trophies, cups, and ribbons everywhere: swimming, archery, football, horseback riding.

Was there nothing my cousin Will couldn't do?

I sat down on the edge of the bed. He can do everything. I can't do anything.

I looked up, and there was my grand-pappy. He knew what was going through my mind.

"Son, we're all gifted for something. Your job is to find out what that gift is, and then get good at it! Words...are...nourishment. They feed your thoughts, so tell yourself, 'I am a mountain!'"

All I could think of was, "How could I tell myself 'I am a mountain' with a nickname like the one my family had given me? Butterbean!" *(audience laughter)*

MCC, FT, Honored Guests...

Sometimes life just deals you cards...that don't add up to much. And if you get bad cards often enough, pretty soon it wears you down...and eventually, you give up on your dreams.

Michael Angelo said, "The greater danger for most of us is not that our aim is too high and we miss it, it's that it's too low...and we reach it."

I went through a period in my life, when my aim was low...and I was reaching it...till I met a man named Jim Armstrong...he showed me how to set my aim high, *and* how to reach it.

I was in his juggling workshop, and I was fed up with dropping the balls all day long. I was sitting off on the side, having my own personal pity party...when Jim came up and said, "Which dog are you feeding?"

"What, there's no dogs here!"

"Oh yes there are. There are two dogs going in your head the whole time! And one dog goes, "You're amazing! You're fantastic! You're the champ! You're the best! Go for it!" *(audience laughter)* and the other one goes, "Who you kidding you worthless maggot? You never amounted to much, and you never will! Why do you even bother?" And at any given time, you'll be feeding one dog...or the other. Now, if you wanna be successful...you've-got-to-feed-the-right-dog! Erick, what do you do for a living?"

"I'm a background extra, but what I *really* want is my name in lights...a big fat check...and I wouldn't mind a new nickname while we're at it!" *(audience laughter)*

"Great! Well have some belief in yourself! Send your resume off to the *biggest* show you can find! And remember...feed the right dog!"

So I did. I sent my resume to the biggest show I could find. I got an audition!

I remember standing at the back of the room...number 1471. The room was full of the *best* acrobats and gymnasts who had come from around the world...to compete. They were all aged 18 or 19. I, on the other hand, was 41! I feel like I'm *eighty-one* compared to these kids! *(audience laughter)*

No, Erick, feed the right dog. What was it grand-pappy said?

"I am a mountain, I have set my inner compass, I'm focused on my dreams, and I will persist until I succeed."

I got through the audition.

Next was a heights test. They took me to an aircraft hangar.

Inside, was a tall carbon fiber pole, one hundred feet high with a crow's nest at the top.

They said, "We're going to winch you to the top, and you're going to stand on the outside of the crow's nest. You're going to move your body-weight, and the pole will sway back and forth...and at the maximum oscillation, you'll become weightless. We want you to do all kinds of acrobatic tricks...Impress us!" *(audience laughter)*

"There's no way on God's Green Earth that Iiiiiiiyyy am-a-MOUNTAIN! I have set my inner compass, I am focused on my goal and I will persist until I succeed!"

I passed that test.

They said, "We really like you Erick. It's down to just you and one other guy...for the starring role!"

Wow, starring role!

"Who is this other guy?"

"His name is Charles Jarman. He's a stuntman on the film Gladiator! He'll be here on Friday at ten o'clock"

Friday, ten o'clock, the door flies open and in walks this *huge*, six foot five Afro-Caribbean man, *really good looking*, pearly white teeth, ripped muscles.

He drops his bag and takes out some nunchukus. [gestures wildly whilst making spinning sounds]

"Hi, I'm Charles!" *(in deep voice) (audience laughter)*

You-have-got-to-be-kidding! This is like David and Goliath! Wait a minute...David won. He must have fed the right dog. I know how to do that!

"Mountain...compass...focus...succeed" *(in stage whisper)*

Charles got the job *(disappointed tone followed by pause for huge audience laughter)*

And so did I. *(audience laughter)*

They liked us both so much they gave us each a starring role!

I got my name in lights, I got a big fat cheque, and they didn't call me Butterbean! *(audience laughter)* They called me "Ion!" *(audience laughter)*

Life is not a dress rehearsal. There are no second chances.

And all along our journey, we have two dogs going in our head and having a tug of war...The one that wins is the one you feed. And in the movie of your life, *you* decide if you're going to be the background extra...or the rising star!

They say when you meet somebody and interact with them in any way, a little piece of them...becomes a part of you.

The part of me that is Grand pappy wants to ask you..."Have you found your gift?"

The part of me that is Michael Angelo wants to know..."Have you set your aim *high?*"

And the part of me that is Jim Armstrong says..."Feed the right dog!"

CHAPTER NINE

HOW TO MESMERIZE YOUR AUDIENCE

"Your purpose is to make your audience see what you saw, hear what you heard, feel what you felt. Relevant detail, couched in concrete, colorful language, is the best way to recreate the incident as it happened and to picture it for the audience."
Dale Carnegie

CAPTURE ATTENTION BY CREATING CURIOSITY

Erick captures audience attention with his opening by creating curiosity:

> Shhh, do you hear that?

> It's a dog growling.

> And another one...panting.

As soon as Erick delivers this opening, what do you think audience members are thinking?

Exactly, they're thinking: "What dogs? I don't hear any dogs!" And just like that, Erick cleverly and subtly hooks his audience members into his speech.

Erick continues to build the curiosity by saying, "everyone in this room is a dog owner … you just don't know it yet".

Again, audience members are thinking, "Really? What is he talking about? I don't own any dogs!"

If you want to hook audience members into your speech, create an opening that generates curiosity.

How do you know if your opening generates curiosity?

Simply look at your opening and ask yourself, "What questions pop into the audience's mind after listening to this opening?"

If your opening causes the audience members to ask questions, you've successfully reeled them into your speech. If, however, your opening fails to generate any questions in your audiences' minds, you need a new opening!

USE VOCAL VARIETY TO SPICE UP YOUR SPEECH

Erick makes great use of vocal variety to keep his audience members engaged. Consider the following sentences from Erick's speech:

I recognize these sounds because...I'm a dog owner. I have two...and they're <u>very</u> hungry and they <u>demand</u> my attention!

This section makes great use of vocal variety. For example, Erick stresses the word "demand" so that it sounds like a dog growling.

In your speeches, place emphasis on key words to convey a feeling or to emphasize the importance of an idea. Vocal variety adds spice to your speeches and keeps your audience members engaged … and awake! A monotone voice (staying at the same level all the way throughout your speech) will result in a bored audience.

Remember, the key to vocal variety is in the <u>variety!</u> If you're always loud and fast, then nothing sticks out. If you're always quiet, then nothing sticks out and your audience members will be hypnotized into sleeping.

The key to being a dynamic speaker is to vary your volume and speed. That means that you need to have some places where you speak loudly, other places where you speak softly … some places where you create excitement and tension by speaking quickly, and other places where you slow down.

SMOOTH TRANSITION INTO THE MAIN BODY OF THE SPEECH

Erick creates a smooth transition between the opening and the main body of his speech:

> Oh, they're not real...they live...up here (gesture pointing to the head)

> I first got an inkling that there was something going on up here (second gesture to head) when I was seven years old.

This transition seamlessly shifts audience attention from the hypothetical dogs to the first story.

Focus on creating smooth transitions between the opening and body of your speech.

(MODIFIED) SUSPENDED STORY

Erick cleverly uses a modified version of the Suspended Story.

Before I explain how Erick used the modified version of the suspended story, let me first explain what the suspended story is. Trust me, you're going to love this structure.

The suspended story is one of my favorite structures. It works like this:

Start Story 1: The speaker starts off with story number 1. When Story #1 reaches the main conflict, the speaker immediately dives into story number 2. In other words, the speaker leaves the conclusion of the story hanging. Audience members are left wondering how Story #1 will be concluded while the speaker dives into Story #2.

Vikas Jhingran, the 2003 World Champion of Public Speaking, used the Suspended Story formula to keep his audience enthralled by his speech. He started with the following story:

> "My hands were shaking. My throat was dry. In my hand was a letter that was going to change my life!
>
> M.I.T. Massachusetts Institute of Technology. The graduate school of my dreams!
>
> Would it be for the better...or for the worse?
>
> The answer...was in my hands!"

See, you're interested in finding out what the letter says, aren't you?

However, instead of revealing what the letter says, Vikas dives into Story #2 with the following transition:

> "My mind and thoughts whirled back to the time when it all began..."

Having a flawless transition into the second story is a must if you're going to use the suspended story formula.

Begin & Wrap Up Story #2: The speaker dives into Story #2. The first and second stories are related in some way, although the second story doesn't give away the conclusion of the first.

In his winning speech, Vikas Jhingran dives into his second story and shares the story of how he used to be a struggling undergraduate student. He takes audience members through the conflict of the second story, shares the guru's wisdom and wraps up Story #2 before he goes back to Story #1.

Conclude Story #1: Vikas finally comes back to Story #1 and gives the conclusion of the first story:

> "Yes, the letter did begin with Congratulations! I had achieved my dream!"

This speech structure keeps audience members constantly intrigued because audience members are always subconsciously wondering how the first story will end. When they do finally find out how the first story concludes, they experience a sense of satisfaction at having solved the mystery.

See, I told you it was a great speech structure!

Can you apply the suspended story formula to your speech?

Now, let's get back to Erick's speech.

Erick uses a *modified* version of the suspended story. His speech doesn't follow the classic suspended story structure, although it does have a "suspended element." Let me explain:

Erick starts off his speech with the hypothetical dogs:

> You're a dog owner, and you're a dog owner.
>
> In fact, everyone is in this room is a dog owner...you just don't know it yet.
>
> I'm going to tell you about my dogs, and then I'm going to introduce you to yours.
>
> Oh, they're not real...they live...up here.

Next, instead of immediately revealing the significance of the dogs, Erick dives into his first story:

> I first got an inkling that there was something going on up here when I was seven years old.
>
> I was visiting my relatives in Tennessee. I walked into my cousin Will's room. There were trophies, cups, and ribbons everywhere: swimming, archery, football, horseback riding.

Instead of revealing what the hypothetical dogs represent, Erick keeps his audience members intrigued to find out how the dogs are related to his speech. The dogs are the "suspended element" in the speech.

We only find out in Erick's second story what the hypothetical dogs represent. When the audience members finally do find out the significance of the dogs, they experience a sense of satisfaction because of having their curiosity fulfilled.

Can you use a "suspended element" in your speech to keep your audience members intrigued throughout your speech?

Can you use a modified version of the suspended story to keep your audience members curious about a particular aspect of your speech?

BE SPECIFIC

When telling a story, be as specific as possible. Instead of saying, "My cousin had lots of awards," be specific and instead say, "There were trophies, cups and ribbons everywhere: swimming, archery, football, horseback riding." The words "trophies, cups and ribbons" create specific mental picture in the audience's minds, whereas the phrase "lots of awards" isn't very effective at conjuring mental images.

By being specific and providing as many relevant details as possible, you paint pictures in your audience's minds and help them mentally "see" your story.

Here's another example of how Erick provides specific details:

> I remember standing at the back of the room...number 1471

Again, notice how specific Erick is. He even recounts the number "1471." When you include these small but specific details, you add credibility to your speech and your speech becomes "real" for your audience members.

In your speeches and presentations, always try to be as specific as possible. Include the specific dates or times to add credibility to your speech.

USE SELF-DEPRECATING HUMOR

As we've seen in the other speeches, self-deprecating humor is the safest form of humor.

> All I could think of was, "How could I tell myself 'I am a mountain' with a nickname like the one my family had given me? Butterbean!"

Don't be afraid to poke a little bit of fun at yourself.

SOFTEN THE BLOW WITH A "WE-FOCUS"

In this section, Erick uses a "You-Focus" to tell the audience:

> ... life just deals you cards that don't add up to much ... and eventually, you give up on your dreams.

While this may be true, it may cause some audience members to think, "No, I don't give up on my dreams!" and turn them off.

I believe that this section would be better with a "We-Focus" instead. So, for example, the above sentence would become:

> Sometimes life just deals us cards that don't add up to much ... and eventually, we give up on our dreams.

I believe that this We-Focus softens the impact of the "blow" because audiences don't like being told negative things about themselves.

QUOTE FOR CREDIBILITY

Using a quote from a well-known person increases the credibility of your speech, which is exactly what Erick does. In his speech, he quotes Michael Angelo:

Michael Angelo said, "The greater danger for most of us is not that our aim is too high and we miss it, it's that it's too low...and we reach it."

Apart from boosting the speech's credibility, this quote also takes on the form of the "guru's wisdom" so that Erick is able to make his point without seeming like a preachy know-it-all. Can you use a quote to provide the wisdom in your speech?

USE AN ORIGINAL ANALOGY

Erick uses an original analogy in his speech.

In this speech, Erick compares the positive and negative thoughts in our heads to a "happy dog" and a "grouchy dog." This analogy works well because it transforms the abstract idea of positive and negative thoughts into a specific mental picture we can see.

Ever since hearing Erick's speech, I've always thought of my negative thoughts as the "grouchy dog" and tried to feed the positive dog instead. By turning an abstract idea into a specific visual (using an analogy), Erick has had an impact on my life.

Turning your abstract ideas into specific visual images makes your message memorable. More importantly, it can help you leave a long-lasting positive impact on your audience's lives.

ESTABLISH THE CONFLICT, INTRODUCE THE GURU, RESOLVE THE CONFLICT

Erick's stories follow the recommended storytelling structure. The stories establish a conflict, introduce a guru and end with the main character overcoming the conflict. Let's look at one of Erick's stories as an example:

> I went through a period in my life, when my aim was low...and I was reaching it...till I met a man named Jim Armstrong...he showed me how to set my aim high, and how to reach it.
>
> I was in his juggling workshop, and I was set up with dropping the balls all day long. I was sitting off on the side, having my own personal pity party...when Jim came up and said, "Which dog are you feeding?"
>
> "What, there's no dogs here!"
>
> "Oh yes there are. There are two dogs going in your head the whole time! And one dog goes, "You're amazing! You're fantastic! You're the champ! You're the best! Go for it!" and the other one goes, "Who you kidding you worthless maggot? You never amounted to much, and you never will! Why do you even bother?" And at any given time, you'd be feeding one dog...or the other. Now, if you wanna be successful...you've-got-to-feed-the-right-dog! Eric, what do you do for a living?"

"I'm a background extra, but what I really want is my name in lights...a big fat check...and I wouldn't mind a new nickname while we're at it!"

"Great! Well have some belief in yourself! Send your resume off to the biggest show you can find! And remember...feed the right dog!"

So I did. I sent my resume to the biggest show I could find. I got an audition!

Great. What's the conflict in this story? The conflict (problem) is that Erick's "aim" in life was too low.

Who's the guru? Jim Armstrong.

What's the guru's wisdom? It's the dialogue with the line "feed the right dog!"

What's the resolution of the first story? Erick sends his resume to the biggest show he can find and gets an audition.

It's a simple, effective storytelling structure that works every time! Of course, it's not the *only* storytelling structure, but it is one of the most effective ones.

Do your stories follow this formula?

KEEP RATCHETING UP THE SUSPENSE BY ESCALATING THE CONFLICT

In this speech, Erick keeps escalating the intensity of the conflicts. Notice how the conflicts in Erick's stories become increasingly tougher to overcome with each story. By escalating the conflicts, Erick keeps his audience members excited and wrapped up in his speech. Let's have a look at how the conflicts become increasingly more intense:

Conflict #1: Low aim in life. Relatively easy to overcome. Erick sends off his résumé to the biggest show and gets an audition.

Conflict #2: Audition against some of the *best* acrobats and gymnasts in the world. Tougher conflict than the first. Plus, the acrobats are younger than Erick, so the odds are stacked against him. However, Erick manages to get through the audition.

Conflict #3: Heights test. Very difficult obstacle to overcome. Erick manages to pass the test.

Conflict #4: Erick's up for the starring role. However, he has to face the most difficult conflict yet. He's competing against a huge, six-foot-five Afro-Caribbean man who was the stuntman on "Gladiator." The odds are most certainly against Erick.

Can you see how the challenges in Erick's path escalate in intensity until the conflict reaches its highest point during his competition against Charles Jarman?

Keep intensifying the conflict in your stories and you'll keep ratcheting up the suspense. Your audience will have no choice but to be completely immersed in your speech.

DESCRIBE YOUR MAIN CHARACTERS IN DETAIL

Charles Jarman is one of the main characters in the speech because he is the biggest obstacle between Erick and his dream. Therefore, Erick spends some time describing Charles Jarman so that the audience can picture him in their minds:

> Friday, ten o'clock, the door flies open and in walks this huge, six foot five Afro-Caribbean man, really good looking, pearly white teeth, ripped muscles.

Again, notice how specific Erick is with his descriptions. Instead of saying "a tall, good-looking, muscular man," Erick uses specific descriptions to help the audience conjure an image of an intimidating man ("six foot five … ripped muscles").

CONNECT THE MESSAGE TO YOUR AUDIENCE

Near the end of the speech, Erick links the message directly to his audience so that they go away from the speech with a valuable lesson.

He says:

> And all along our journey, we have two dogs going in our head and having a tug of war...The one that wins is the one you feed. And in the movie of your life, you decide if you're going to be the background extra...or the rising star!

How are you connecting your story and your message to your audience?

TAKE AN ELEMENT OUT OF YOUR SPEECH AND PUT IT INTO YOUR AUDIENCE'S LIFE

Erick's speech is all about his journey from being a background extra to becoming a rising star. Notice how he takes this particular element from his speech and puts it into his audience's life using an appropriate metaphor ("in the movie of your life"):

> And in the movie of your life, you decide if you're going to be the background extra...or the rising star!

Most of the audience members listening to Erick's speech aren't trying to become acrobats and gymnasts. However, by taking the element of "background extra" and "rising star" out of his speech and applying it to his audience's life, Erick allows his audience members to reflect on their own goals and dreams. Erick's background-extra-to-rising-star story becomes a springboard from which audience members can reflect on their own lives.

Let me give you another example of how you can take an element out of your speech and put it into your audience's life.

In one my speeches about avoiding Dream killers (negative people), I talk about my ex-girlfriend. Here's a small section of the speech:

> After high school, my dream was to start a business.
>
> So when my brilliant business idea popped into my head, I couldn't wait to share it with my friends!
>
> So I shared it…with my ex-girlfriend…
>
> Nancy Negative listened to my idea and said, "What do you know about running a business?"
>
> Very encouraging, isn't she? (audience laughter)
>
> See, there's a reason she's my ex! (audience laughter)

Later on in the speech, I take the element of "Nancy Negative" and apply it to the audience's life. I say:

> Who is your Nancy Negative?
>
> Who's holding you back?
>
> Get rid of the Nancy Negatives in your life and you'll be able to accomplish far more than you ever thought was possible!

Do you see how my ex-girlfriend, Nancy Negative, now becomes a metaphor for all the negative people in my audience members' lives?

Later on in the speech, I explain that getting rid of negative people was just one step towards achieving my dream. A second step was to get rid of the negative thoughts I was carrying around in my head:

> I began to take stock of the thoughts and ideas and beliefs I was carrying around inside my head.
>
> And you know what I realized?
>
> My head was full of Nancy Negatives!
>
> Although I'd gotten rid of Nancy from my life, I was still carrying around in my head with my own personal Nancy Negative.
>
> And you know what the worst thing was?

She just wouldn't shut up! (audience laughter)

Are you carrying around a Nancy Negative in your head?

Do you see how I turned Nancy Negative into a metaphor for my inner critic? And do you see how I took that out of my speech and applied it to my audience's lives by asking them about their inner Nancy Negative?

In your next speech, remember to take an element out of your speech and apply it to your audience's lives to get them to reflect on their life.

CREATIVELY SUMMARIZE YOUR MAIN POINTS/GET YOUR AUDIENCE TO REFLECT BY ASKING THEM QUESTIONS

Erick does a brilliant job of summarizing his three main points. He summarizes his main points as questions directed to the audience so that his audience members can reflect on lessons that he learned:

The part of me that is Grand pappy wants to ask you..."Have you found your gift?" The part of me that is Michael Angelo wants to know..."Have you set your aim high?" And the part of me that is Jim Armstrong says..."Feed the right dog!"

SPEAKING TOOLKIT SUMMARY #4
ACTIONABLE KNOWLEDGE

Speak clearly, if you speak at all; carve every word before you let it fall.
Oliver Wendell Holmes

- Capture attention by creating curiosity in your opening
- Use vocal variety to spice up your speech
- Create smooth transitions
- Use the (modified) suspended story/element to keep your audience intrigued
- Be specific
- Use self-deprecating humor
- Soften the blow with a We-Focus
- Quote for credibility
- Use an original analogy
- Establish the conflict, escalate the conflict, introduce the guru, resolve the conflict
- Keep ratcheting up the suspense by increasing the intensity of your conflicts
- Describe your main characters in detail
- Connect the message to your audience

- Take an element out of your speech and put it into your audience's lives
- Creatively summarize your main points
- End by asking questions and getting your audience to reflect on your message

CHAPTER TEN

WRAP UP: HOW TO KEEP YOUR AUDIENCE ENGAGED WITH STORIES

"Storytelling reveals meaning without committing the error of defining it."
Hannah Arendt

You've read and analysed speeches by four of the best speakers on the planet. You've evaluated each speech line-by-line and studied what makes each speech effective. You've learned how to tell compelling, irresistible stories that keep your audience hooked onto your every word. By now, you've picked up close to one hundred advanced tools and techniques on the art of public speaking and storytelling.

Because there are so many tools covered in this tiny book, this chapter will serve as a useful checklist when you next craft your speech or presentation.

Here's a quick list of all the public speaking and storytelling tools covered in this book. I suggest that you come back and read this list several weeks later to refresh your memory:

35 PUBLIC SPEAKING AND STORYTELLING TIPS TO MAKE YOUR NEXT SPEECH AN OUTSTANDING ONE

1. Your opening should create questions in your audience's minds. It should get them curious about your speech/story.

2. Start off with a BOOM! Begin your speech in the middle of the most exciting part of your story.

3. If you're struggling to find a story, look for stories in your everyday life. Which personal story do you most often share with your friends? What transformative experience have you gone through which has taught you most about life?

4. Realize that your story doesn't have to make people cry. It can make people laugh or simply think. However, it must cause some kind of emotional shift in your listeners.

5. The conflict is the heart of the story. Introduce the problem/conflict early on in the story.

6. Use the suspended story structure (or a modified version of it) to keep your audience in suspense.

7. Keep ratcheting up the suspense by escalating the intensity of the conflicts.

8. Your story must have a guru or a "catalyst for change". Don't be the hero of your own story.

9. If you have too many "gurus"/ "catalysts for change", choose just one of them to represent them all.

10. Add humor to your story to keep your audience engaged. The secret to humor is to create an expectation and then break it.

11. Customize your humor for your audience.

12. Use self-deprecating humor to lighten the mood. Don't be afraid to poke fun at yourself.

13. Look for humor opportunities within dialogue.

14. Use anchors to make your points memorable. Every time you make a point, anchor it with an anecdote, acronym, activity or analogy.

15. Use analogies and metaphors to make your speech memorable for your audience.

16. Ensure smooth transitions between different parts of your story.

17. Give your audience dialogue/verbalize what they are thinking to build a stronger connection with them.

18. Use beautiful, vivid descriptions to bring the scenes in your stories to life for your audience.

19. Give enough description of your main characters so that your audience can picture them in their heads.

20. Provide specific details to add credibility to your story.

21. Use a quote to add credibility to your speech.

22. Use tough-watch logic to inspire your audience.

23. Inspire people by talking about people who inspire you.

24. Use vocal variety to spice up your speech. Adjust your pitch and pace to reflect the characters voices and the mood of your story.

25. Use the singular you-focus to have a one-on-one conversation with your audience.

26. Keep linking your message and your story to your listeners using you-focused check-ins

27. Take an element out of your speech and put it into your audience's life to keep your story relevant to them

28. There must be a resolution to the conflict in your speech.

29. Your characters must change as a result of the conflict

30. The resolution to the conflict must provide a carryout message for your audience ("Tell a story and make a point")

31. Turn your carryout message into a short memorable catchphrase you can repeat several times throughout your speech to make your message stick

32. It's important to end your speech with a bang. Consider closing your speech with audience participation.

33. Creatively summarize your main points and get your audience to reflect by asking them questions

34. Another option to end your speech is to use a circular closing that ties in beautifully with your opening

35. End your speech with a key takeaway message and a next step for your audience

QUESTIONS OR COMMENTS?

I'd love to hear your thoughts. Email me at:
akash.speaker@gmail.com

INTERESTED IN HAVING ME SPEAK AT YOUR NEXT EVENT?

I deliver high-impact keynotes and workshops on productivity, time-management, success psychology and effective communication. Check out the full list of my training programs on www.AkashKaria.com/Keynotes and reach me on akash.speaker@gmail.com to discuss how we can work together.

GRAB $297 WORTH OF FREE RESOURCES

Want to learn the small but powerful hacks to make you insanely productive?

Want to discover the scientifically proven techniques to ignite your influence?

Interested in mastering the art of public speaking and charisma?

Then head over to www.AkashKaria.com to grab your free "10X Success Toolkit" (free MP3s, eBooks and videos designed to unleash your excellence).

Be sure to sign up for the newsletter and join over 11,800 of your peers to receive free, exclusive content that I don't share on my blog: www.AkashKaria.com

YOU MIGHT ALSO ENJOY

If you enjoyed this book, then check out Akash's other books (and see what other readers are saying).

HOW TO DESIGN TED-WORTHY PRESENTATION SLIDES

The Phenomenal No.1 Amazon Bestseller

"A great resource...I have been teaching workshops at universities and Fortune 500 Campuses up and down the East Coast on building better presentations. Akash hits all the right notes in this book. A must read for anyone wanting to build powerful presentations."~ David Bishop

"I will admit to rarely reviewing books. However, this book was such a step above any others I've read on the art of PowerPoint presentations, I had to give it a five star review. I have already recommended this book on my blog and will keep it in my ready reference...!"
~ David Schwind

Get the book on Amazon:

www.AkashKaria.com/TEDPresentation

HOW TO DELIVER A GREAT TED TALK: PRESENTATION SECRETS OF THE WORLD'S BEST SPEAKERS

"Why can some speakers grab the attention of an audience and keep them spellbound throughout their entire presentation, but most fall flat on their faces and are quickly forgotten? Akash has captured the best ideas, tools, and processes used by some of the best speakers and presenters in the world. He has distilled them in to a step-by-step, easy-to-read guide that will help you discover, develop, and deliver presentations which help you stand out from the crowd…Whether you are a new speaker learning the art of speaking, or a veteran looking for a new perspective, How to Deliver a Great TED Talk is a wise investment that can help take your speaking to a higher level."
~ Michael Davis, Certified World Class Speaking Coach

"I waited quite a while to read this book, and now that I have, I wish I would have opened it sooner. Fantastic information and easy to follow format."
~ Noell Beadelia

Get the book on Amazon:
www.AkashKaria.com/TEDTalkBook

READY, SET...PROCRASTINATE! 23 ANTI-PROCRASTINATION TOOLS DESIGNED TO HELP YOU STOP PUTTING THINGS OFF AND START GETTING THINGS DONE

"This is one book you should not delay reading! Having struggled with procrastination for much of my life, Akash Karia's book came like a breath of fresh air. He provides clear, practical advice on how to overcome the problem, but warns that you will need to work at it daily. If there is just one thing that you should not put off, it is reading this book."
~ Gillian Findlay

Get the book on Amazon:
www.AkashKaria.com/AntiProcrastination

PERSUASION PSYCHOLOGY: 26 POWERFUL TECHNIQUES TO PERSUADE ANYONE!

"I'm a huge fan of Akash's writing style and the way he can distill quite a complex subject into concise bite-sized points you can take away and convert into action. The book covers many different aspects of persuasion from the way you look to the words you use."
~ Rob Cubbon, author of "From Freelancer to Entrepreneur"

Get the book on Amazon:
www.AkashKaria.com/Persuasion

ANTI NEGATIVITY: HOW TO STOP NEGATIVE THINKING AND LEAD A POSITIVE LIFE

"Akash is a master at taking complex ideas and communicating with simplicity and brilliance. He honors your time by presenting what you need to know right away, and follows up with some excellent examples as reinforcement. If you're looking for some simple and effective ways to stop thinking negatively and a new season of positivity, definitely check out this book."
~ Justin Morgan

Get the book on Amazon:
www.AkashKaria.com/AntiNegativity

WANT MORE?

Then check out Akash's author-page on Amazon:
www.bit.ly/AkashKaria

ABOUT THE AUTHOR

Akash Karia is an award winning speaker and peak-productivity coach who has been ranked as one of the Top Ten speakers in Asia Pacific. He is an in-demand international speaker who has spoken to a wide range of audiences including bankers in Hong Kong, students in Tanzania, governmental organizations in Dubai and yoga teachers in Thailand. He currently lives in Tanzania where he works as the Chief Commercial Officer of a multi-million dollar company.

"If you want to learn presentation skills, public speaking or just simply uncover excellence hidden inside of you or your teams, **Akash Karia is the coach to go to.**" ~ *Raju Mandhyan, TV show host, Expat Insights, Philippines*

"Akash Karia is a fine public speaker who knows his subject very well. He has an immense understanding in what it takes for a successful presentation to pull through. **A rare talent who has much in store for you as an individual, and better yet, your organization.**" ~ *Sherilyn Pang, Business Reporter, Capital TV, Malaysia*

Voted as one of the "**10 online entrepreneurs you need to know in 2015**" by *The Expressive Leader*

Featured as one of the "**top 9 online presentations of 2014**" by *AuthorStream.com*

Akash is available for speaking engagements and flies from Tanzania. Contact him for coaching and training through his website: www.AkashKaria.com

CONNECT WITH AKASH

Get your Free Speaking Toolkit on:
www.AkashKaria.com

Check out more awesome books:
www.bit.ly/AkashKaria

Email for speaking-related inquires:
akash@akashkaria.com / akash.speaker@gmail.com

Connect on Facebook:
www.facebook.com/PublicSpeakingCoach

Connect on LinkedIn:
www.LinkedIn.com/In/AkashKaria

50809007R00080

Made in the USA
Lexington, KY
31 March 2016